A Spiritual Formation Journal

A Spiritual Formation Journal

A RENOVARÉ Resource for Spiritual Renewal

Created by Jana Rea
with Richard J. Foster

HarperSanFrancisco
An Imprint of HarperCollins*Publishers*

For information about RENOVARÉ, write to RENOVARÉ, 8 Inverness Drive East, Suite 102, Englewood, CO 80112–5609.

Icons on "Reflection and Report" and "Plan and Practice" pages created by Greg May.

To my family,
Shapers of our history.

CONTENTS

Acknowledgments

To THOSE who have gone before me and to those who came alongside me in the making of this journal, I offer my heartfelt thanks.

Greg Shannon, Tracy Zoeller, Cindy Cook, Rita Linnens, Ron Goodman, Chris Penny, Art Thomas, and Lynda Graybeal were there when I needed them.

Debbie Mullen, Al Gregg, Beth Rea, and the staff at Eighth Day Books were research angels.

A special couple, Maurice and Peggy Roberts, cheered me on with prayers and words of encouragement.

More than a decade of fellowship with the friends in "House Church," Al and Joyce Gregg, Glen and Joyce Veenstra, Bob and Nancy Rozzelle, and Dave and Janice McClintock, provided the inspiration for this journal as well as the lab in which to try it out.

To Kandace Hawkinson, the editor who listened to an idea and gave a new writer a chance, I will be forever grateful.

Finally, to my family, Ed, Beth, and Chad, for their constant prayers, affection, and good humor.

My sincere appreciation to all.

Jana Rea

FOREWORD

YOU ARE unique. Utterly, totally, completely unique. Me too. No one experiences your experiences in the same way that you do. And because you are unique, you have a story to tell. A unique story, a one-of-a-kind story. And one of the best ways you have of discovering your story and telling your story is through journal writing.

Journal writing is reflective writing. By ruminating on the events and experiences, frustrations and joys of your days, you enable the original you to emerge. This unique you has been there all the time; reflective journal writing does not produce your uniqueness. But it can uncover this uniqueness, much as the process of tumbling and cutting and polishing reveals a stone's varied hues and unique patterns.

True, the story may be told only to yourself . . . and to God. But then, isn't that audience enough? The "audience of One" is really all that counts. And God is great enough and good enough to receive all your telling. The angers. The secrets. The fears. The sorrows. The wonderings. The hopes. The ecstasies. He is big enough for it all.

So write away. Tell the story, the unique story, your story.

Richard J. Foster
September 1995

INTRODUCTION

A *Spiritual Formation Journal* is for all who desire a more attentive and intentional spiritual life. For centuries journal writing has been used to bring the inner life into focus for examination and celebration. By means of reflection upon events, circumstances, and relationships, journal writing encourages an inner dialogue that promotes growth. This practice provides the pause necessary to see what is easily overlooked. In a journal, mysteries of the heart unfold.

My own journal writing began with my third-grade diary. The carefully guarded binder, complete with lock and key, was my introduction into a habit sustained now by many years and hundreds of spiral notebooks. My journals chronicle my story; they make me realize first of all that I have a story to share, if only with myself. But most of all, they are touchstones, altars where I meet God within me.

Journal writing has been called "spiritual autobiography." Michael Blumenthal describes the raw material from which we each mold and shape our story: "Deep down in some long-encumbered self, it is the story you have been writing all of your life."[1] With our desire to explore aspects of our lives reflectively, creatively, and prayerfully, our journal writing becomes a record of our inner quest for meaning, and our search for God. Dan Wakefield, in *The Story of Your Life,* refers to this simultaneous process as a "pilgrimage to look for the source of one's faith and see one's experience in relation to that search, . . . writing about our search is 'a way to do theology.' "[2] In *Our Many Selves,* Elizabeth O'Connor explores the notion that we are only able to grow in our relationship with God to the extent that we are willing to know ourselves. "Though by and large the Church has not known how integral the search for self is to the search for God, her saints have always preached that the two are inextricably bound together."[3] John Calvin writes, "Our wisdom, in so far as it ought to be deemed true and solid wisdom, consists almost entirely of two parts: the knowledge of God and of ourselves. But as these are connected together by many ties, it is not easy to determine which of the two precedes, and gives birth to the other."[4] As a youth I heard the Methodist evangelist Tommy Tyson say, "There are parts of me that haven't even heard of Jesus yet!" Reconciling "our parts" to God seems to be a lifelong undertaking.

Where we begin our journey of faith in one sense is where we remain—with our multifaceted self, and with an unfathomable God.

And so our journal will contain a blend of discovery. It is a safe place to do exploration, shed our misconceptions, reclaim our lost or forgotten parts, recover the fragments that living makes of us at times, and cultivate the gift of new life. In this way, journal writing becomes a viable prayer form, and our journal our own book of psalms. In the privacy of personal reflection, insights are received, confessions are offered, progress is noted. Journal writing fosters a careful attention to our soul's condition, and we are better for the tending.

In all of life there are seasons to observe. A journal nurtures respect for the passage of time, allowing us to sense our own inner rhythm or dance with life. As the cycles of nature enact their pageantry of birth and death, they can prompt realization of the soul's need to celebrate a beginning or mourn an ending. At such times a journal becomes a tool, a camera that frames our life, dividing it into manageable segments.

Inner questions often emerge in the process. A good question always has a prodding quality that is invaluable to our faith. And a good journal tracks these questions even if they remain unanswered for years. As author James Newby notes, "In matters of faith there will always be questions. Learning to love the questions while living in faith is the creative tension where spiritual growth takes place."[5] Reflective questions pave new highways within; they break up the concrete of old, restrictive thinking so God's Spirit can flow. "I have learned to write and describe to the Father in journal form my hardness of soul and spirit," says Gordon MacDonald. He continues, "Usually after three or more paragraphs of frank talk, I find the inner stone begins to break up."[6]

God promises in Ezekiel, "I will remove the heart of stone from their flesh and give them a heart of flesh, so that they may follow my statutes and keep my ordinances and obey them. Then they shall be my people, and I will be their God" (11:19b–20). Journals are a record or landmark in this redemption process. They keep us accountable on a daily basis, expectant and watchful for redemptive possibilities in each new day.

Most often this redemptive work is done in the context of a caring community; it does not happen solely in isolation. Whether it is a church or a small group, we all need safe places to be heard and known as we are . . . and as we hope to be.

Often when we cannot see God at work in our own life, we are strengthened by evidence of his Presence in others who candidly share their joys and struggles. Where one is weak, another is strong for a friend's sake. In this fellowship with other, very human beings, we find a place of commonality in our desire to grow in our faith. Together, with time and patience, we slowly develop the skill of recognizing the good hand of God. The psalmist declares, "I would have lost heart unless I had believed that I would see the goodness of the LORD in the land of the living" (Ps. 27:13, NKJV). Encouragement always comes when we catch glimpses of God at work on our behalf. And that is often seen most clearly in the eyes and lives of those who also seek him.

This is why *A Spiritual Formation Journal* is designed for both individual and small-group use. In fact, this resource grew out of my experience in one such group when I recognized the need for a good tool to track our spiritual journeys from week to week. The journal brings focus to the events of the week and helps each member prepare to share. It also provides space to keep a record of the prayer requests and personal endeavors of others in a way that adds continuity and accountability. The beauty in this ordinary give-and-take of community life is discovering Christ himself who has promised to be among us.

Even when we have the best intentions, spiritual maturity eludes us without a model. That need is satisfied in Jesus Christ. But often, without our even realizing it, our perception of Jesus is colored by our particular persuasion or denomination. This condition can inhibit growth rather than promote it. Church history is littered with the debris of splits and splinters among the richly diverse people of God. As in all conflict, the potential for growth is present, but we seem to need a way of viewing Christ with the objectivity needed to grow beyond our own experience.

In response to this widespread hunger for a fuller vision of Christ among us, RENOVARÉ was born. Founded by Richard J. Foster, RENOVARÉ (Latin meaning "to make new") brings together the best spiritual treasures from several great Christian traditions to challenge our ingrown tendencies and encourage a more balanced practice of our faith. RENOVARÉ focuses on five traditions: Contemplative, Holiness, Charismatic, Social Justice, and Evangelical. While all of these can be seen in various denominational forms, they also reflect significant aspects of Christ's life and offer a pattern for spiritual growth. Balance comes from blending these time-honored traditions. RENOVARÉ resources promote an understanding of these streams of faith; *A Spiritual Formation Journal* provides a place to work the understanding in and flesh it out.

My own journey through the denominational halls of Christendom made me more than ready for such a perspective. Raised on a denominational battleground between a Catholic father and a Protestant mother, I have longed for a sanctuary where both of these persuasions could be given honor in expression. Since childhood the longing remains, and, in fact, I have learned that these are by no means the only two camps in conflict. Throughout my Christian life I've experienced the cross fire over doctrinal disputes and the deep wounds that result when fellowship is denied. Perplexed, I've repeatedly read the testimony offered in Ephesians, "For He Himself is our peace, who made both groups into one, and broke down the barrier of the dividing wall . . . thus establishing peace, and . . . reconcil[ing] them both in one body to God through the Cross" (2:14–16, NASV).

The peace and unity described here had always seemed to me an ideal beyond realization, a reality for heaven only. Then I discovered RENOVARÉ, and slowly its vision began to make sense to me. For the first time in my life I began to see that, somewhat like river tributaries that water their God-given paths, denominations through the years have served the very human purpose of honoring our differences, even our preferences. At the same time, the various streams—each unique, each essential—magnify an aspect of God's character and his desired work on earth. A contemplative life is a prayer-filled life; holiness concerns itself with the practice of virtue; a charismatic life focuses on spiritual sensitivity; social justice gives attention to matters of human need; and the evangelical life centers on the word of God and the work of evangelism.

As Christians seeking to be conformed to the image of Christ, we can expect to find God at work on our behalf in each of these areas. But just as the various muscles of our bodies respond with varying degrees of strength to physical tasks, we may be able to respond to some areas of God's work more easily than others. For instance, compassionate, outgoing individuals might easily engage in service or evangelism while finding it a challenge to develop a meaningful devotional life. On the other hand, more contemplative persons may need a nudge into situations that are beyond their comfort zone, ones that require a more public use of a gift like teaching. Courage to exercise new "muscles" comes from seeing the qualities operative in each other and at the same time being willing to scrutinize our own prejudices. The benefit is two-sided: a healthier community, to be sure, but also a deeper respect for our differences. Respect always precedes reconciliation. A holy dynamic permeates our entire lives as we are reconciled to God, to ourselves, and to each other. Whenever and wherever that happens, we experience harbingers of heaven; in small ways, the kingdom comes.

Navigating this kind of philosophic and relational change is no small feat. Self-awareness is an anchor that helps us maintain a sane estimate of ourselves in the process. This journal provides a place to begin, a place to explore new dimensions of faith and exercise new disciplines with the hope that, as we do, we will "grow up in every way into him who is the head, into Christ" (Eph. 4:15).

Divided into weekly sections, *A Spiritual Formation Journal* offers five lined pages each week for notations. A blank page entitled "Stirrings" provides less structured, more free-flowing space for a drawing or a poem or the recollection of a meaningful conversation. These pages can be a place to acknowledge a soul ache, record a dream, or marvel at a glimpse of God in an unorthodox place. They may very well be an incubator where life can grow in the warm, safe climate of God's brooding Presence, unseen by human eyes, unannounced until its time. Woven throughout the fabric of this journal are quotes and queries to encourage reflection and expression. They are not meant to be imposing, only inviting.

Each weekly section ends with the opportunity to evaluate the week, note the experiences of others on the journey with us, and design a plan for the next week. Whether or not you are formally in a group, or whether or not your group officially follows the RENOVARÉ format, does not matter. This journal is equally valuable for personal accountability. It can be used as creatively as you choose.

At best, *A Spiritual Formation Journal* is a travel log for the spiritual journey, a tracking tool to note progress, a sketchbook for the development of ideas into actions. It is a diary for that special ongoing dialogue between God and you; a very personal history book waiting to be written, waiting to be lived.

Jana Rea

NOTES

1. Michael Blumenthal, "The New Story of Your Life," *Against Romance* (New York: Viking, 1987), p. 83.
2. Dan Wakefield, *The Story of Your Life* (Boston: Beacon, 1990), pp. 5, 7.
3. Elizabeth O'Connor, *Our Many Selves* (New York: Harper & Row, 1971), p. 103.
4. John Calvin, Institutes of the Christian Religion, vol. 1, trans. Henry Beveridge (Grand Rapids, MI: Eerdmans, 1981), p. 37.
5. James Newby, "A Questioning People," *Quaker Life* (January/February 1993): 4.
6. Gordon MacDonald, "Soul Talk," *Discipleship Journal* (March/April 1994): 34.

Our favourite distinction between the spiritual life and the practical life is false. We cannot divide them. One affects the other all the time; for we are creatures of sense and of spirit, and must live an amphibious life.

Evelyn Underhill

Self-knowledge *puts us on our knees, and it
is very necessary for love. For knowledge of
God gives love, and knowledge of self
gives humility.*

Mother Teresa of Calcutta

❧

Wherever I am deluded,
   I welcome now your spirit of Truth;
Wherever I have chosen to hide,
   seek me out.
I would be found by You.

❧

*Lord, show me myself; let me respect and
love my inward man, and then I shall be
ready for the King of Glory to come in. And
in time I shall learn to bow before the inner
man in all men.*

Josephine Moffett Benton

❧

The "religious act" is always something
partial; "faith" is something whole, involving
the whole of one's life. Jesus calls men,
not to a new religion, but to life.

Dietrich Bonhoeffer

❧

Stirrings

Today as I picture Jesus holding my face cupped in his hands, and holding my gaze to his—am I ashamed? Do I want to turn away? Can I fully receive his love for me?

REFLECTION AND REPORT

In what ways is God making his Presence known to me?

_____

_____

_____

_____

What difficulty or success did I encounter while seeking holiness of heart and life?

_____

_____

_____

What spiritual gifts did the Spirit enable me to exercise?

_____

_____

What opportunities did I have to serve others or work for peace and justice?

_____

_____

_____

How has Scripture shaped the way I think and live?

_____

_____

Spiritual Formation Group

Name _____

_____

_____

_____

Name _____

_____

_____

_____

Name _____

_____

_____

_____

Name _____

_____

_____

_____

Name _____

_____

_____

_____

Name _____

_____

_____

_____

PLAN AND PRACTICE

I will set aside time regularly for prayer, meditation, and spiritual reading and will seek to practice the Presence of God.

_____
_____
_____
_____

By God's grace I will strive mightily against sin and will do deeds of love and mercy that lead to righteousness.

_____
_____
_____
_____

I will seek the gifts of the Holy Spirit, nurturing the fruit and experiencing the joy and power of the Spirit.

_____
_____
_____
_____

I will seek to serve others everywhere I can and will work for justice in all human relationships and social structures.

_____
_____
_____
_____

I will study the Scriptures regularly and share my faith with others as God leads.

_____
_____
_____
_____

It has pleased the Lord to teach me a truth. . . . I saw more clearly than ever that the first great and primary business to which I ought to attend every day was, to have my soul happy in the Lord.

George Müller

I have chosen the way of faithfulness.

Psalm 119:30

Where do I need to learn faithfulness?
Express faithfulness?

❧

The Christian stands, not under the dictator-
ship of a legalistic "You ought," but in the
magnetic field of Christian freedom, under
the empowering of the "You may."

Helmut Thielicke

❧

The place God calls you to is the place where
your deep gladness and the world's deep
hunger meet.

Frederick Buechner

❧

The first requirement of religion is that we accept the laws of life. The spiritual life consists only in a series of new births. There must be new flowerings, new prophets, new adventures—always new adventures—if the heart of man, albeit in fits and starts, is to go on beating.

Paul Tournier

❧

Stirrings

There are many doors in my soul—
Which ones are shut?

REFLECTION AND REPORT

In what ways is God making his Presence known to me?

_____

_____

_____

_____

What difficulty or success did I encounter while seeking holiness of heart and life?

_____

_____

_____

_____

What spiritual gifts did the Spirit enable me to exercise?

_____

_____

_____

_____

What opportunities did I have to serve others or work for peace and justice?

_____

_____

_____

_____

How has Scripture shaped the way I think and live?

_____

_____

_____

_____

Spiritual Formation Group

Name _____

_____

_____

_____

Name _____

_____

_____

_____

Name _____

_____

_____

_____

Name _____

_____

_____

_____

Name _____

_____

_____

_____

Name _____

_____

_____

_____

PLAN AND PRACTICE

I will set aside time regularly for prayer, meditation, and spiritual reading and will seek to practice the Presence of God.

_____

_____

_____

_____

By God's grace I will strive mightily against sin and will do deeds of love and mercy that lead to righteousness.

_____

_____

_____

_____

I will seek the gifts of the Holy Spirit, nurturing the fruit and experiencing the joy and power of the Spirit.

_____

_____

_____

_____

I will seek to serve others everywhere I can and will work for justice in all human relationships and social structures.

_____

_____

_____

_____

I will study the Scriptures regularly and share my faith with others as God leads.

_____

_____

_____

_____

*Lord, I am yours; I do yield myself up entirely
to you, and I believe that you accept me.
I leave myself with you. Work in me all the
good pleasure of your will, and I will only lie
still in your hands and trust you.*

Hannah Whitall Smith

☙

May the God of peace himself sanctify you entirely; and may your spirit and soul and body be kept sound and blameless at the coming of our Lord Jesus Christ.

1 Thessalonians 5:23

How do I glorify God in my body?
Am I listening to my body's needs?
What patterns or rhythms does my body
need in order to be responsive to God?

❧

Energy and enthusiasm come from true
recognition of God's active Presence in my
life. Forgive me, God, when complacency
renders me unaware of your Presence.
Awake me to praise.

❧

Social concern is the dynamic Life of God at
work in the world . . . particularized in each
individual or group who is sensitive and
tender in the leading-strings of love.

Thomas Kelly

The faith of Christ does not parallel the world, it intersects it. In coming to Christ we do not bring our old life up onto a higher plane; we leave it at the cross.

A. W. Tozer

Stirrings

Work is not always required of a man. There is such a thing as sacred idleness,
the cultivation of which is now fearfully neglected.

George MacDonald

REFLECTION AND REPORT

In what ways is God making his Presence known to me?

_____

_____

_____

_____

What difficulty or success did I encounter while seeking holiness of heart and life?

_____

_____

_____

What spiritual gifts did the Spirit enable me to exercise?

_____

_____

_____

What opportunities did I have to serve others or work for peace and justice?

_____

_____

_____

How has Scripture shaped the way I think and live?

_____

_____

_____

SPIRITUAL FORMATION GROUP

Name

Name

Name

Name

Name

Name

PLAN AND PRACTICE

 I will set aside time regularly for prayer, meditation, and spiritual reading and will seek to practice the Presence of God.

_____

_____

_____

_____

 By God's grace I will strive mightily against sin and will do deeds of love and mercy that lead to righteousness.

_____

_____

_____

 I will seek the gifts of the Holy Spirit, nurturing the fruit and experiencing the joy and power of the Spirit.

_____

_____

_____

 I will seek to serve others everywhere I can and will work for justice in all human relationships and social structures.

_____

_____

_____

 I will study the Scriptures regularly and share my faith with others as God leads.

_____

_____

_____

The Day's First Job

With every morn my life afresh must break
The crust of self, gathered about me fresh.

George MacDonald

❧

Virtues meditated on but not practiced some-
times inflate our minds and courage and we
think that we really are such as we have
thought and resolved to be.

Francis de Sales

❧

Am I allowing my spiritual life to be frittered away, or am I bringing it all to one centre— the Atonement of my Lord? Is Jesus Christ more and more dominating every interest in my life? If the one central point, the great exerting influence in my life is the Atonement of the Lord, then every phase of my life will bear fruit for Him.

Oswald Chambers

If we believe in the Incarnation of the
Son of God,
there should be no one on earth
in whom we are not prepared to see,
in mystery,
the presence of Christ.

Thomas Merton

Renewal of the mind requires acknowledging
that we must study diligently in order to
understand the truth and respond faithfully
to what is revealed to us. In the long run,
depth of commitment must be supported by a
corresponding depth of understanding.

Kathryn A. Yanni

❧

Stirrings

What happens to a dream deferred?
Does it dry up
like a raisin in the sun?
or fester like a sore—
and then run?

Langston Hughes

REFLECTION AND REPORT

 In what ways is God making his Presence known to me?

_____

_____

_____

_____

 What difficulty or success did I encounter while seeking holiness of heart and life?

_____

_____

_____

_____

 What spiritual gifts did the Spirit enable me to exercise?

_____

_____

_____

_____

 What opportunities did I have to serve others or work for peace and justice?

_____

_____

_____

_____

 How has Scripture shaped the way I think and live?

_____

_____

_____

_____

SPIRITUAL FORMATION GROUP

Name _____

_____

_____

_____

Name _____

_____

_____

_____

Name _____

_____

_____

_____

Name _____

_____

_____

_____

Name _____

_____

_____

_____

Name _____

_____

_____

_____

PLAN AND PRACTICE

 I will set aside time regularly for prayer, meditation, and spiritual reading and will seek to practice the Presence of God.

_____

_____

_____

_____

 By God's grace I will strive mightily against sin and will do deeds of love and mercy that lead to righteousness.

_____

_____

_____

_____

 I will seek the gifts of the Holy Spirit, nurturing the fruit and experiencing the joy and power of the Spirit.

_____

_____

_____

_____

 I will seek to serve others everywhere I can and will work for justice in all human relationships and social structures.

_____

_____

_____

_____

 I will study the Scriptures regularly and share my faith with others as God leads.

_____

_____

_____

_____

Stand at the crossroads, and look,
and ask for the ancient paths,
where the good way lies; and walk in it,
and find rest for your souls.

Jeremiah 6:16

❧

Now to Him who is able to keep you
from stumbling,
And to present you faultless
Before the presence of His glory with
exceeding joy,
To God our Savior,
Who alone is wise,
Be glory and majesty,
Dominion and power,
Both now and forever.
Amen.

Jude 24 (NKJV)

What do I stumble over?

Humility is the balance between the truth
about weakness and confidence in the
infinite mercy of God.

Thomas Keating

❧

The more we are able to face our own
capacity for evil the less likely we
are to spread the disease.

Alan Jones

☙

*A Christian is one who, among other things,
admits daily that he has done those things
which he ought not to have done and left
undone those things which he ought to
have done. . . . He cries out in sincerity,
"God be merciful to me a sinner."*

D. Elton Trueblood

Stirrings

When we are able to keep company with our own fears and sorrows, we are shown the way to go; our own parched lives are watered and the earth becomes a greener place.

Elizabeth O'Connor

REFLECTION AND REPORT

In what ways is God making his Presence known to me?

_____
_____
_____
_____

What difficulty or success did I encounter while seeking holiness of heart and life?

_____
_____
_____
_____

What spiritual gifts did the Spirit enable me to exercise?

_____
_____
_____
_____

What opportunities did I have to serve others or work for peace and justice?

_____
_____
_____
_____

How has Scripture shaped the way I think and live?

_____
_____
_____
_____

Spiritual Formation Group

Name _____

_____

_____

Name _____

_____

_____

Name _____

_____

_____

Name _____

_____

_____

Name _____

_____

_____

Name _____

_____

_____

PLAN AND PRACTICE

 I will set aside time regularly for prayer, meditation, and spiritual reading and will seek to practice the Presence of God.

_____

_____

_____

 By God's grace I will strive mightily against sin and will do deeds of love and mercy that lead to righteousness.

_____

_____

_____

 I will seek the gifts of the Holy Spirit, nurturing the fruit and experiencing the joy and power of the Spirit.

_____

_____

_____

 I will seek to serve others everywhere I can and will work for justice in all human relationships and social structures.

_____

_____

_____

 I will study the Scriptures regularly and share my faith with others as God leads.

_____

_____

_____

Nature and God—I neither knew
Yet Both so well knew me
They startled, like Executors
Of My identity.

Emily Dickinson

Because he knows me so well, in what ways
is God making his Presence known to me?

❧

Jesus did not agonize over motives of service nor attempt to explain the mystery of pain and suffering. He set about to open men's eyes that they might see beauty, to open their ears that they might hear truth, to heal the brokenhearted and to make the sick whole. He calls us to do the same.

Josephine Moffett Benton

In our love of people are we to be excitedly hurried, sweeping all men and tasks into our concern? No, that is God's function. But He, working within us, portions out His vast concern into bundles, and lays on each of us our portion. These become our tasks. Life from the Center is a heaven-directed life.

Thomas Kelly

The seed, the sprout, the blossom,
and the seed-bearing fruit—
Help me to tend well
each planting of your Spirit within me.

❧

When we enter upon the spiritual life, we should consider and examine to the bottom what we are.

Brother Lawrence

Stirrings

Often care of the soul means not taking sides when there is a conflict at a deep level. It may be necessary to stretch the heart wide enough to embrace contradiction and paradox.

Thomas Moore

REFLECTION AND REPORT

 In what ways is God making his Presence known to me?

_____

_____

_____

_____

 What difficulty or success did I encounter while seeking holiness of heart and life?

_____

_____

_____

_____

 What spiritual gifts did the Spirit enable me to exercise?

_____

_____

_____

_____

 What opportunities did I have to serve others or work for peace and justice?

_____

_____

_____

_____

 How has Scripture shaped the way I think and live?

_____

_____

_____

_____

SPIRITUAL FORMATION GROUP

Name _____

_____

_____

_____

Name _____

_____

_____

_____

Name _____

_____

_____

_____

Name _____

_____

_____

_____

Name _____

_____

_____

_____

Name _____

_____

_____

_____

PLAN AND PRACTICE

I will set aside time regularly for prayer, meditation, and spiritual reading and will seek to practice the Presence of God.

_____

_____

_____

By God's grace I will strive mightily against sin and will do deeds of love and mercy that lead to righteousness.

_____

_____

_____

I will seek the gifts of the Holy Spirit, nurturing the fruit and experiencing the joy and power of the Spirit.

_____

_____

_____

I will seek to serve others everywhere I can and will work for justice in all human relationships and social structures.

_____

_____

_____

I will study the Scriptures regularly and share my faith with others as God leads.

_____

_____

_____

What I needed was the solitude to expand in breadth and depth and to be simplified out under the gaze of God more or less the way a plant spreads out its leaves in the sun.

Thomas Merton

❧

Create in me a clean heart, O God,
  and put a new and right spirit within me.

Psalm 51:10

What of God's Spirit do I try to give
without first receiving it into my own soul?

౭ఌ

Modern psychology has made us aware that we become individuals in relationship with others and that where there is no genuine community the self is damaged and grows in crooked ways. . . . When the Church wakes again it will know that there can be no consequential change in the lives of people unless there is community.

Elizabeth O'Connor

*For it is not mere words that nourish the soul
but God Himself, and unless and until the
hearers find God in personal experience they
are not the better for having heard the truth.
The Bible is not an end in itself, but a means
to bring men to an intimate and satisfying
knowledge of God, that they may enter into
Him . . . that they may delight in His
Presence, may taste and know the inner
sweetness of the very God Himself in
the core and center of their hearts.*

A. W. Tozer

Stirrings

Spirituality is seeded, germinates, sprouts and blossoms in the mundane. It is to be found and nurtured in the smallest of daily activities.

Thomas Moore

REFLECTION AND REPORT

In what ways is God making his Presence known to me?

_____
_____
_____
_____

What difficulty or success did I encounter while seeking holiness of heart and life?

_____
_____
_____
_____

What spiritual gifts did the Spirit enable me to exercise?

_____
_____
_____
_____

What opportunities did I have to serve others or work for peace and justice?

_____
_____
_____
_____

How has Scripture shaped the way I think and live?

_____
_____
_____
_____

SPIRITUAL FORMATION GROUP

Name _____

_____

_____

_____

Name _____

_____

_____

_____

Name _____

_____

_____

_____

Name _____

_____

_____

_____

Name _____

_____

_____

_____

Name _____

_____

_____

_____

PLAN AND PRACTICE

 I will set aside time regularly for prayer, meditation, and spiritual reading and will seek to practice the Presence of God.

_____
_____
_____
_____

 By God's grace I will strive mightily against sin and will do deeds of love and mercy that lead to righteousness.

_____
_____
_____

 I will seek the gifts of the Holy Spirit, nurturing the fruit and experiencing the joy and power of the Spirit.

_____
_____
_____

 I will seek to serve others everywhere I can and will work for justice in all human relationships and social structures.

_____
_____
_____

 I will study the Scriptures regularly and share my faith with others as God leads.

_____
_____
_____

You cannot, by pure self-discipline, renew your own spirit. This is God's responsibility. Yours is to be still, to listen, to relax. God is at work and will refresh and recreate as you give Him time and attention.

Luci Shaw

The disciple is one who, intent upon becoming Christlike and so dwelling in his "faith and practice," systematically and progressively rearranges his affairs to that end. By these actions, even today, one enrolls in Christ's training, becomes his pupil or disciple. There is no other way.

Dallas Willard

❧

All we do under the impulse of fear does not bear the fruits of the Spirit. The deep-rooted realization that God is our Abba drives out fear.

Peter van Breeman

❧

*It is not the religious act that makes the
Christian, but participation in the suffering
of God in the secular life . . . living unre-
servedly in life's duties, problems, successes
and failures, experiences and perplexities. In
so doing we throw ourselves completely
into the arms of God.*

Dietrich Bonhoeffer

❧

Christian faith is never faith in faith.
Christian faith is never without content.
Christian faith is never a jump in the dark.
Christian faith is always believing what God
has said. And Christian faith rests upon
Christ's finished work on the cross.

Francis Schaeffer

Stirrings

Oh God
what are you doing
   in the basement of my soul?
I ask
because I sense
the shifting and moving
of foundational rocks
that have borne my life's weight;
structures of Belief.
I ask because I would trust
the earth and rock-moving circumstances
if I could know for sure
it is you.

REFLECTION AND REPORT

In what ways is God making his Presence known to me?

_____
_____
_____
_____

What difficulty or success did I encounter while seeking holiness of heart and life?

_____
_____
_____

What spiritual gifts did the Spirit enable me to exercise?

_____
_____
_____
_____

What opportunities did I have to serve others or work for peace and justice?

_____
_____
_____

How has Scripture shaped the way I think and live?

_____
_____
_____
_____

And when all my hopes in them and in all
men were gone, so that I had nothing out-
wardly to help me, nor could tell what to do,
then, Oh then, I heard a voice which said,
"There is one, even Christ Jesus, that can
speak to thy condition," and when I heard
it my heart did leap for joy.

George Fox

It is not what you are nor what you have
been that God looks at with his merciful eyes,
but what you desire to be.

The Cloud of Unknowing

❧

Compassion is such a deep, central and
powerful emotion in Jesus that it can only be
described as a movement of the womb of
God. There, all the divine tenderness and
gentleness lies hidden. There, God is father
and mother, brother and sister, son and
daughter. There, all feelings, emotions, and
passions are one in divine love.

Henri Nouwen

Praise to you
Spirit of fire!
to you who sound the timbrel
and the lyre.
Your music sets our minds ablaze! The
    strength of our souls
awaits your coming
in the tent of meeting.

Hildegard of Bingen

☙

Stirrings

You must meet Him, who can on any day,
Fashion Love from ordinary clay.

Calvin Miller

Before evangelism is a program, it is a
passion—a passion of the heart which
issues in saving action.

Leighton Ford

✌

Plan and Practice

I will set aside time regularly for prayer, meditation, and spiritual reading and will seek to practice the Presence of God.

_____

_____

_____

By God's grace I will strive mightily against sin and will do deeds of love and mercy that lead to righteousness.

_____

_____

_____

I will seek the gifts of the Holy Spirit, nurturing the fruit and experiencing the joy and power of the Spirit.

_____

_____

_____

I will seek to serve others everywhere I can and will work for justice in all human relationships and social structures.

_____

_____

_____

I will study the Scriptures regularly and share my faith with others as God leads.

_____

_____

_____

Spiritual Formation Group

Name _____

_____

_____

_____

Name _____

_____

_____

_____

Name _____

_____

_____

_____

Name _____

_____

_____

_____

Name _____

_____

_____

_____

Name _____

_____

_____

_____

REFLECTION AND REPORT

In what ways is God making his Presence known to me?

_____

_____

_____

_____

What difficulty or success did I encounter while seeking holiness of heart and life?

_____

_____

_____

What spiritual gifts did the Spirit enable me to exercise?

_____

_____

_____

What opportunities did I have to serve others or work for peace and justice?

_____

_____

_____

How has Scripture shaped the way I think and live?

_____

_____

_____

Spiritual Formation Group

Name _____

_____

_____

_____

Name _____

_____

_____

_____

Name _____

_____

_____

_____

Name _____

_____

_____

_____

Name _____

_____

_____

_____

Name _____

_____

_____

_____

PLAN AND PRACTICE

I will set aside time regularly for prayer, meditation, and spiritual reading and will seek to practice the Presence of God.

_____

_____

_____

By God's grace I will strive mightily against sin and will do deeds of love and mercy that lead to righteousness.

_____

_____

_____

I will seek the gifts of the Holy Spirit, nurturing the fruit and experiencing the joy and power of the Spirit.

_____

_____

_____

I will seek to serve others everywhere I can and will work for justice in all human relationships and social structures.

_____

_____

_____

I will study the Scriptures regularly and share my faith with others as God leads.

_____

_____

_____

Men may tire themselves in a labyrinth of search, and talk of God; but if we would know him indeed, it must be from the impressions we receive of him: and the softer our hearts are, the deeper and livelier those will be upon us.

William Penn

Pride cuts us off from love; lying, from truth;
and despair, from mercy. All three see to it
that we freeze to death.

Alan Jones

It is not what a man does that determines whether his work is sacred or secular, it is why he does it. The motive is everything. Let a man sanctify the Lord God in his heart and he can thereafter do no common act.

A. W. Tozer

Little children, let us love, not in word or speech, but in truth and action.

1 John 3:18

Where can my words and actions create a deed of love today? What have I said I would do that I haven't yet done?

☙

You can never give another person that which
you have found, but you can make him
homesick for what you have.

Oswald Chambers

❧

Stirrings

It is the heart that is not yet sure of its God that is afraid to laugh in His presence.

George MacDonald

REFLECTION AND REPORT

 In what ways is God making his Presence known to me?

_____

_____

_____

_____

 What difficulty or success did I encounter while seeking holiness of heart and life?

_____

_____

_____

 What spiritual gifts did the Spirit enable me to exercise?

_____

_____

_____

 What opportunities did I have to serve others or work for peace and justice?

_____

_____

_____

 How has Scripture shaped the way I think and live?

_____

_____

_____

Spiritual Formation Group

Name _____

_____

_____

_____

Name _____

_____

_____

_____

Name _____

_____

_____

_____

Name _____

_____

_____

_____

Name _____

_____

_____

_____

Name _____

_____

_____

_____

PLAN AND PRACTICE

 I will set aside time regularly for prayer, meditation, and spiritual reading and will seek to practice the Presence of God.

_____

_____

_____

_____

 By God's grace I will strive mightily against sin and will do deeds of love and mercy that lead to righteousness.

_____

_____

_____

_____

 I will seek the gifts of the Holy Spirit, nurturing the fruit and experiencing the joy and power of the Spirit.

_____

_____

_____

_____

 I will seek to serve others everywhere I can and will work for justice in all human relationships and social structures.

_____

_____

_____

_____

 I will study the Scriptures regularly and share my faith with others as God leads.

_____

_____

_____

_____

Come, my people, enter your chambers,
And shut your doors behind you;
Hide yourself, as it were, for a little moment.

Isaiah 26:20 (NKJV)

Know that the ancient Enemy strives by all means to hinder your desire to do good, and to keep you void of all religious exercises.

Thomas à Kempis

❧

O Christian soul! If you do not find in your-
self the strength to worship God in spirit and
in truth; if your heart does not yet feel the
warmth and sweetness of mental interior
prayer, then bring to prayer that sacrifice
which you can, which is in the power of your
will and your strength. Let your lips first
become familiar with frequent, uninter-
rupted prayerful calling; let them constantly,
without interruption call on the powerful
name of Jesus Christ.

The Way of a Pilgrim

❦

*Intercession is not only the best arbitrator of
all differences, the best promoter of true
friendship, the best cure and preservative
against all unkind tempers, all angry and
haughty passions; it is also of great use to
discover to us the true state of
our own hearts.*

William Law

❧

We are put on earth for a little space that we may learn to bear the beams of love.

William Blake

Stirrings

If I were an open field—
What would I like to see growing there?
What would I build there?

REFLECTION AND REPORT

In what ways is God making his Presence known to me?

_____

_____

_____

_____

What difficulty or success did I encounter while seeking holiness of heart and life?

_____

_____

_____

What spiritual gifts did the Spirit enable me to exercise?

_____

_____

_____

What opportunities did I have to serve others or work for peace and justice?

_____

_____

_____

How has Scripture shaped the way I think and live?

_____

_____

_____

SPIRITUAL FORMATION GROUP

Name _____

_____

_____

_____

Name _____

_____

_____

_____

Name _____

_____

_____

_____

Name _____

_____

_____

_____

Name _____

_____

_____

_____

Name _____

_____

_____

_____

PLAN AND PRACTICE

I will set aside time regularly for prayer, meditation, and spiritual reading and will seek to practice the Presence of God.

_____
_____
_____
_____

By God's grace I will strive mightily against sin and will do deeds of love and mercy that lead to righteousness.

_____
_____
_____

I will seek the gifts of the Holy Spirit, nurturing the fruit and experiencing the joy and power of the Spirit.

_____
_____
_____

I will seek to serve others everywhere I can and will work for justice in all human relationships and social structures.

_____
_____
_____

I will study the Scriptures regularly and share my faith with others as God leads.

_____
_____
_____

Like leftovers, day after day
my prayers are tasteless.
Satisfy me with your mercies
that are new every morning.

❧

People who think that they are spiritually superior because they make a practice of a discipline such as fasting or silence or frugality are entirely missing the point. The need for extensive practice of a given discipline is an indication of our weakness, not our strength. . . . The disciplines we need to practice are precisely the ones we are not "good at."

Dallas Willard

*The Holy Spirit is not a luxury meant to
make deluxe Christians, . . . the Spirit is an
imperative necessity. Only the Eternal
Spirit can do eternal deeds.*

A. W. Tozer

He has told you, O mortal, what is good;
and what does the LORD require of you
but to do justice, and to love kindness,
and to walk humbly with your God?

Micah 6:8

Here is the Gospel message in all its original simplicity, undyingly new: the message that men and women are really loved by God, that sins are really forgiven and that the mercy of God, beyond all our comprehension, has come to drive out forever the bitterness of selfish hearts and fill us instead with the sweetness of His presence forever.

Thomas Merton

❧

Stirrings

Who despises the day of small things?

Zechariah 4:10 (NIV)

Is there a small step or a beginning in my life that I need to celebrate?

REFLECTION AND REPORT

 In what ways is God making his Presence known to me?

_____

_____

_____

_____

 What difficulty or success did I encounter while seeking holiness of heart and life?

_____

_____

_____

_____

 What spiritual gifts did the Spirit enable me to exercise?

_____

_____

_____

_____

 What opportunities did I have to serve others or work for peace and justice?

_____

_____

_____

_____

 How has Scripture shaped the way I think and live?

_____

_____

_____

_____

Spiritual Formation Group

Name _____

_____

_____

_____

Name _____

_____

_____

_____

Name _____

_____

_____

_____

Name _____

_____

_____

_____

Name _____

_____

_____

_____

Name _____

_____

_____

_____

PLAN AND PRACTICE

I will set aside time regularly for prayer, meditation, and spiritual reading and will seek to practice the Presence of God.

_____

_____

_____

_____

By God's grace I will strive mightily against sin and will do deeds of love and mercy that lead to righteousness.

_____

_____

_____

_____

I will seek the gifts of the Holy Spirit, nurturing the fruit and experiencing the joy and power of the Spirit.

_____

_____

_____

_____

I will seek to serve others everywhere I can and will work for justice in all human relationships and social structures.

_____

_____

_____

_____

I will study the Scriptures regularly and share my faith with others as God leads.

_____

_____

_____

_____

God is a Person, and in the deep of His mighty nature He thinks, wills, enjoys, feels, loves, desires and suffers as any other person may. In making Himself known to us He stays by the familiar pattern of personality. He communicates with us through the avenues of our minds, our wills and our emotions. The continuous and unembarrassed interchange of love and thought between God and the soul . . . is the throbbing heart of [the] New Testament.

A. W. Tozer

The question of forming habits on the basis of the grace of God is a very vital one. . . . If we refuse to practice, it is not God's grace that fails when a crisis comes, but our own nature. When the crisis comes, we ask God to help us, but He cannot if we have not made our nature our ally. The practicing is ours, not God's. God regenerates us and puts us in contact with all His divine resources, but He cannot make us walk according to His will.

Oswald Chambers

*No limit can be set on our progress towards
God: first because no limitation can be put
upon the beautiful, and secondly because the
increase in our desire for the beautiful cannot
be stopped by any sense of satisfaction.*

Gregory of Nyssa

❧

If we would be truly free and at home, we are
to share in the life of a God who weeps, who
suffers, who identifies with the poorest and
most wretched among us. The question . . . is,
Do you really want to share in the life
of such a God?

Alan Jones

No aspect of thinking on conversion is more foreign to the American evangelical experience than this stress on conversion as a process. . . . Evangelicals emphasize emotion and an initial movement. This moment is celebrated, recalled, and when the experience fades, recaptured. But Christian tradition does not agree. . . . Conversion is a continuous and lifelong process. Conversions proceed layer by layer, relationship by relationship, here a little, there a little—until the whole personality, intellect, feeling, and will have been recreated by God.

John H. Westerhoff

Stirrings

Because loneliness is the brooding parent
Of becoming—thought and busy being
Seldom come together.

Calvin Miller

REFLECTION AND REPORT

In what ways is God making his Presence known to me?

_____

_____

_____

What difficulty or success did I encounter while seeking holiness of heart and life?

_____

_____

_____

What spiritual gifts did the Spirit enable me to exercise?

_____

_____

_____

What opportunities did I have to serve others or work for peace and justice?

_____

_____

_____

How has Scripture shaped the way I think and live?

_____

_____

_____

SPIRITUAL FORMATION GROUP

Name

Name

Name

Name

Name

Name

PLAN AND PRACTICE

I will set aside time regularly for prayer, meditation, and spiritual reading and will seek to practice the Presence of God.

_____

_____

_____

By God's grace I will strive mightily against sin and will do deeds of love and mercy that lead to righteousness.

_____

_____

_____

_____

I will seek the gifts of the Holy Spirit, nurturing the fruit and experiencing the joy and power of the Spirit.

_____

_____

_____

I will seek to serve others everywhere I can and will work for justice in all human relationships and social structures.

_____

_____

_____

I will study the Scriptures regularly and share my faith with others as God leads.

_____

_____

_____

Draw your shield about me, Lord.
Let me feel the protection
of your Faith while mine grows.

❧

Oh to grace, how great a debtor

Daily I'm constrained to be!

Let thy goodness, like a fetter,

bind my wandering heart to Thee.

Prone to wander,

Lord, I feel it

Prone to leave the God I love:

Here's my heart,

Oh take and seal it

Seal it for thy courts above.

Robert Robinson

Follow me.

Mark 2:14

Such a simple invitation. What life-changing response does it require today? Where do I need more power to obey?

✲

We must learn to regard people less in light of what they do, or omit to do, and more in the light of what they suffer. The only profitable relationship to others—and especially to our weaker brethren—is one of love, and that means the will to hold fellowship with them. God himself did not despise humanity but became man for men's sake.

Dietrich Bonhoeffer

*Perhaps the challenge of the gospel lies pre-
cisely in the invitation to accept a gift for
which we can give nothing in return. For the
gift is the life breath of God himself, the
Spirit who is poured out on us through Jesus
Christ. This life breath frees us from fear and
gives us new room to live. A man who
prayerfully goes about his life is constantly
ready to receive the breath of God, and to let
his life be renewed and expanded.*

Henri Nouwen

❧

Stirrings

Be patient toward all that is unsolved in your heart and try to love the questions themselves *like locked rooms and like books that are written in a very foreign tongue. Do not
now seek the answers, which cannot be given you because you would not be able to live
them. And the point is, to live everything.* Live *the questions now. Perhaps you will then
gradually, without noticing it, live along some distant day into the answer.*

Rainer Maria Rilke

REFLECTION AND REPORT

In what ways is God making his Presence known to me?

_____

_____

_____

_____

What difficulty or success did I encounter while seeking holiness of heart and life?

_____

_____

_____

_____

What spiritual gifts did the Spirit enable me to exercise?

_____

_____

_____

_____

What opportunities did I have to serve others or work for peace and justice?

_____

_____

_____

_____

How has Scripture shaped the way I think and live?

_____

_____

_____

_____

SPIRITUAL FORMATION GROUP

Name

Name

Name

Name

Name

Name

PLAN AND PRACTICE

 I will set aside time regularly for prayer, meditation, and spiritual reading and will seek to practice the Presence of God.

_____

_____

_____

 By God's grace I will strive mightily against sin and will do deeds of love and mercy that lead to righteousness.

_____

_____

_____

 I will seek the gifts of the Holy Spirit, nurturing the fruit and experiencing the joy and power of the Spirit.

_____

_____

_____

 I will seek to serve others everywhere I can and will work for justice in all human relationships and social structures.

_____

_____

_____

 I will study the Scriptures regularly and share my faith with others as God leads.

_____

_____

_____

Finally let us become accustomed to recollect
ourselves, during the day and in the course of
our duties, by a single look toward God. Let
us thus quiet all the movements of our hearts,
as soon as we see them agitated. Let us sepa-
rate ourselves from all pleasure which does
not come from God. Let us cut off all futile
thoughts and dreams. Let us not speak empty
words. Let us seek God within us and we
shall find him without fail, and with
him joy and peace.

François Fénelon

The road to holiness necessarily passes
through the world of action.

Dag Hammarskjöld

❧

Nondiscipleship costs abiding peace, a life penetrated throughout by love, faith that sees everything in the light of God's overriding governance for good, hopefulness that stands firm in the most discouraging of circumstances, power to do what is right and withstand the forces of evil. In short, it costs exactly that abundance of life Jesus said he came to bring (John 10:10).

Dallas Willard

Christ's cross is Christ's way to Christ's

crown.

William Penn

❧

The guidance and support of a soul seeking
closer communion with God is, I suppose, . . .
the most delicate and responsible work with
which one can be entrusted.

Evelyn Underhill

❧

Stirrings

What more could have been done for my vineyard
than I have done for it?

Isaiah 5:4 (NIV)

What does God long to do in the vineyard of my soul?
Am I ready to give my consent?

REFLECTION AND REPORT

In what ways is God making his Presence known to me?

_____
_____
_____
_____

What difficulty or success did I encounter while seeking holiness of heart and life?

_____
_____
_____

What spiritual gifts did the Spirit enable me to exercise?

_____
_____

What opportunities did I have to serve others or work for peace and justice?

_____
_____
_____

How has Scripture shaped the way I think and live?

_____
_____
_____

Spiritual Formation Group

Name _____
_____
_____
_____

Name _____
_____
_____
_____

Name _____
_____
_____
_____

Name _____
_____
_____
_____

Name _____
_____
_____
_____

Name _____
_____
_____
_____

PLAN AND PRACTICE

I will set aside time regularly for prayer, meditation, and spiritual reading and will seek to practice the Presence of God.

_____

_____

_____

By God's grace I will strive mightily against sin and will do deeds of love and mercy that lead to righteousness.

_____

_____

_____

I will seek the gifts of the Holy Spirit, nurturing the fruit and experiencing the joy and power of the Spirit.

_____

_____

_____

I will seek to serve others everywhere I can and will work for justice in all human relationships and social structures.

_____

_____

_____

I will study the Scriptures regularly and share my faith with others as God leads.

_____

_____

_____

If you would know God, and worship and serve God as you should do, you must come to the means he has ordained and given for that purpose. Some seek it in books, some in learned men; but what they look for is in themselves, though not of themselves; but they overlook it. The Voice is too still, the seed too small, and the light shineth in darkness. Wherefore, O Friends, turn in, turn in, I beseech you. There you want Christ, and there you must find Him.

William Penn

❦

O my soul, . . . be prepared to meet him who
knows how to ask questions.

T. S. Eliot

✌

*All outward power that we exercise in the
things about us is but as a shadow in com-
parison of that inward power that resides in
our will, imagination and desires. These
communicate with eternity and kindle a life
which always reaches heaven or hell.*

William Law

What matters is whether Christians will dare to risk everything in order to fulfill their function in the world.

Jacques Ellul

❧

I have treasured the words of his mouth
more than my daily bread.

Job 23:12 (NIV)

Stirrings

We die daily. Happy those who daily come to life as well.

George MacDonald

REFLECTION AND REPORT

In what ways is God making his Presence known to me?

_____
_____
_____
_____

What difficulty or success did I encounter while seeking holiness of heart and life?

_____
_____
_____
_____

What spiritual gifts did the Spirit enable me to exercise?

_____
_____
_____
_____

What opportunities did I have to serve others or work for peace and justice?

_____
_____
_____
_____

How has Scripture shaped the way I think and live?

_____
_____
_____
_____

SPIRITUAL FORMATION GROUP

Name

Name

Name

Name

Name

Name

Plan and Practice

I will set aside time regularly for prayer, meditation, and spiritual reading and will seek to practice the Presence of God.

_____

_____

_____

By God's grace I will strive mightily against sin and will do deeds of love and mercy that lead to righteousness.

_____

_____

_____

I will seek the gifts of the Holy Spirit, nurturing the fruit and experiencing the joy and power of the Spirit.

_____

_____

_____

I will seek to serve others everywhere I can and will work for justice in all human relationships and social structures.

_____

_____

_____

I will study the Scriptures regularly and share my faith with others as God leads.

_____

_____

_____

Preparation: 1. Place yourself in the presence of God. 2. Beseech Him to inspire you. . . . After completing your prayer, go back over it for a moment and out of the considerations you have made, gather a little devotional bouquet to refresh you during the rest of the day.

Francis de Sales

❧

Christian, fear not to claim God's promises to make thee holy. Listen not to the suggestion that the corruption of the old nature would render holiness an impossibility: . . . The evil nature is there, with its unchanged tendency to rise up and show itself. But the new nature is there too—the living Christ, thy sanctification is there—and through Him all thy powers can be sanctified as they rise unto life, and be made to bear fruit to the glory of the Father.

Andrew Murray

Ascribe to the LORD, *O families of the peoples,*
ascribe to the LORD *glory and strength.*
Ascribe to the LORD *the glory due his name;*
bring an offering, and come before him.
Worship the LORD *in holy splendor.*

1 Chronicles 16:28–29

What offering can I make to the Lord that
will cost me something?

๙

Divine love imposeth no rigorous or unrea-
sonable commands, but graciously points out
the spirit of brotherhood and the way to
happiness, in attaining which it is necessary
that we relinquish all that is selfish.

John Woolman

❦

You made us for yourself, and our heart is restless until it find rest in you.

Augustine

☙

Stirrings

This is the irrational season
When love blooms bright and wild.
Had Mary been filled with reason
There'd have been no room for the child.

Madeleine L'Engle

REFLECTION AND REPORT

In what ways is God making his Presence known to me?

_____
_____
_____
_____

What difficulty or success did I encounter while seeking holiness of heart and life?

_____
_____
_____

What spiritual gifts did the Spirit enable me to exercise?

_____
_____

What opportunities did I have to serve others or work for peace and justice?

_____
_____
_____

How has Scripture shaped the way I think and live?

_____
_____
_____

Spiritual Formation Group

Name _____

_____

_____

_____

Name _____

_____

_____

_____

Name _____

_____

_____

_____

Name _____

_____

_____

_____

Name _____

_____

_____

_____

Name _____

_____

_____

_____

PLAN AND PRACTICE

I will set aside time regularly for prayer, meditation, and spiritual reading and will seek to practice the Presence of God.

By God's grace I will strive mightily against sin and will do deeds of love and mercy that lead to righteousness.

I will seek the gifts of the Holy Spirit, nurturing the fruit and experiencing the joy and power of the Spirit.

I will seek to serve others everywhere I can and will work for justice in all human relationships and social structures.

I will study the Scriptures regularly and share my faith with others as God leads.

Deep within us all there is an amazing inner sanctuary of the soul, a holy place, a Divine Center, a speaking Voice, to which we may continuously return. Eternity is at our hearts, pressing upon our time-torn lives, warming us with intimations of an astounding destiny, calling us home unto Itself.

Thomas Kelly

❧

When the soul is darkened by impure thoughts, you can overcome them by frequently calling on the name of Jesus. You will not find a more powerful and successful tool than this either in heaven or on earth.

John Climacus

For the Mighty One has done
great things for me,
and holy is his name.

Luke 1:49

*Forgiveness is God's invention for coming to
terms with a world in which, despite their
best intentions, people are unfair to each
other and hurt each other deeply. He began
by forgiving us. And he invites us all to
forgive each other.*

Lewis B. Smedes

❦

A Christ not in us is the same thing as a Christ not ours. If we are only so far with Christ as to own and receive the history of his birth, person and character, if this is all that we have of him, we are as much without him as those evil spirits which cried out "we know thee, who thou art, thou holy one of God." It is the language of Scripture that Christ in us is our hope of glory, that Christ formed in us, growing and raising his own life and spirit in us, is our holy salvation.

William Law

Stirrings

I called on the LORD in distress;
The LORD answered me and set me in a broad place.

Psalm 118:5 (NKJV)

What would a "broad place" look like for me?

REFLECTION AND REPORT

In what ways is God making his Presence known to me?

_____
_____
_____
_____

What difficulty or success did I encounter while seeking holiness of heart and life?

_____
_____
_____
_____

What spiritual gifts did the Spirit enable me to exercise?

_____
_____
_____
_____

What opportunities did I have to serve others or work for peace and justice?

_____
_____
_____
_____

How has Scripture shaped the way I think and live?

_____
_____
_____
_____

SPIRITUAL FORMATION GROUP

Name

Name

Name

Name

Name

Name

PLAN AND PRACTICE

 I will set aside time regularly for prayer, meditation, and spiritual reading and will seek to practice the Presence of God.

_____

_____

_____

 By God's grace I will strive mightily against sin and will do deeds of love and mercy that lead to righteousness.

_____

_____

_____

 I will seek the gifts of the Holy Spirit, nurturing the fruit and experiencing the joy and power of the Spirit.

_____

_____

_____

 I will seek to serve others everywhere I can and will work for justice in all human relationships and social structures.

_____

_____

_____

 I will study the Scriptures regularly and share my faith with others as God leads.

_____

_____

_____

So we begin where we are, by getting all the
parts of ourselves working together smoothly
so we're free to move forward.

Alexandra Stoddard

❧

Do not rejoice over me, O my enemy;

    when I fall, I shall rise;

when I sit in darkness,

    the LORD will be a light to me.

Micah 7:8

But thou wilt sin and grief destroy;
That so the broken bones may joy
And tuned together in a well set song
　　Full of his praises,
　　Who dead men raises
Fractures well cured make us more strong.

· George Herbert

❧

In what ways do I act as if God prefers me
over others?*

&

*This query was inspired by the novel *Ellen Foster* by
Kaye Gibbons (Chapel Hill, NC: Algonquin, 1987),
which is rich in social justice themes.

Man's chief end is to glorify God and enjoy Him forever.

Westminster Shorter Catechism

Stirrings

Those seeking the life of the spirit should be cheerful and free, and not neglect recreation.

Teresa of Ávila

REFLECTION AND REPORT

In what ways is God making his Presence known to me?

_____

_____

_____

_____

What difficulty or success did I encounter while seeking holiness of heart and life?

_____

_____

_____

What spiritual gifts did the Spirit enable me to exercise?

_____

_____

_____

What opportunities did I have to serve others or work for peace and justice?

_____

_____

_____

How has Scripture shaped the way I think and live?

_____

_____

_____

SPIRITUAL FORMATION GROUP

Name _____

_____

_____

_____

Name _____

_____

_____

_____

Name _____

_____

_____

_____

Name _____

_____

_____

_____

Name _____

_____

_____

_____

Name _____

_____

_____

_____

PLAN AND PRACTICE

I will set aside time regularly for prayer, meditation, and spiritual reading and will seek to practice the Presence of God.

_____

_____

_____

_____

By God's grace I will strive mightily against sin and will do deeds of love and mercy that lead to righteousness.

_____

_____

_____

I will seek the gifts of the Holy Spirit, nurturing the fruit and experiencing the joy and power of the Spirit.

_____

_____

_____

I will seek to serve others everywhere I can and will work for justice in all human relationships and social structures.

_____

_____

_____

I will study the Scriptures regularly and share my faith with others as God leads.

_____

_____

_____

God is the friend of silence. . . . See how nature, the trees, the flowers, the grass grow in deep silence. See how the stars, the moon and the sun move in silence. The more we receive in our silent prayer, the more we can give in our active life.

Mother Teresa of Calcutta

The ordinary purification and healing, whether of the body or of the mind, takes place only little by little, by passing from one degree to another with labor and patience. The angels upon Jacob's ladder had wings; yet they flew not, but ascended and descended in order from one step to another. The soul that rises from sin to devotion may be compared to the dawning of the day, which at its approach does not expel the darkness instantaneously but only little by little.

Francis de Sales

Living out of the center enables me to speak
and act from greater strength, to heal and
forgive rather than hold grudges, to be capa-
ble of greatness of heart when confronted
with pettiness, to discover that the only valid
reason for doing the right thing is because
it is the right thing.

Brennan Manning

❧

Unclench your fists
Hold out your hands.
Take mine
Let us hold each other
thus is his Glory
Manifest.

Madeleine L'Engle

❧

Oh, you who desire a deeper walk with God,
come enter into His presence
through His Word.

Madame Guyon

Stirrings

If I were a tree, what kind would I be?

REFLECTION AND REPORT

In what ways is God making his Presence known to me?

_____

_____

_____

_____

What difficulty or success did I encounter while seeking holiness of heart and life?

_____

_____

_____

_____

What spiritual gifts did the Spirit enable me to exercise?

_____

_____

_____

_____

What opportunities did I have to serve others or work for peace and justice?

_____

_____

_____

_____

How has Scripture shaped the way I think and live?

_____

_____

_____

_____

SPIRITUAL FORMATION GROUP

Name

Name

Name

Name

Name

Name

PLAN AND PRACTICE

I will set aside time regularly for prayer, meditation, and spiritual reading and will seek to practice the Presence of God.

_____

_____

_____

By God's grace I will strive mightily against sin and will do deeds of love and mercy that lead to righteousness.

_____

_____

_____

I will seek the gifts of the Holy Spirit, nurturing the fruit and experiencing the joy and power of the Spirit.

_____

_____

_____

I will seek to serve others everywhere I can and will work for justice in all human relationships and social structures.

_____

_____

_____

I will study the Scriptures regularly and share my faith with others as God leads.

_____

_____

_____

As thou art in church or cell, that same frame of mind carry into the world, into its turmoil and its fitfulness.

Meister Eckhart

❧

*Be grateful as your deeds become less and less
associated with your name, as your feet ever
more lightly tread the earth.*

Dag Hammarskjöld

❧

Those who have the gale of the Holy Spirit go forward, even in sleep.

Brother Lawrence

Vicit agnus noster, eum sequamur.

Our Lamb has conquered; him let us follow.

John Howard Yoder

You will trust God only as much as you love
Him. And you will love Him not because you
have studied Him; you will love Him because
you have touched Him—in response
to His touch.

Brennan Manning

☙

Stirrings

And here are some more of my reflections;
Yes, I am as full as the moon at the full!

Ecclesiasticus 39:12 (NJB)

REFLECTION AND REPORT

In what ways is God making his Presence known to me?

_____

_____

_____

_____

What difficulty or success did I encounter while seeking holiness of heart and life?

_____

_____

_____

What spiritual gifts did the Spirit enable me to exercise?

_____

_____

_____

What opportunities did I have to serve others or work for peace and justice?

_____

_____

_____

How has Scripture shaped the way I think and live?

_____

_____

_____

Spiritual Formation Group

Name _____
_____
_____
_____

Name _____
_____
_____
_____

Name _____
_____
_____
_____

Name _____
_____
_____
_____

Name _____
_____
_____
_____

Name _____
_____
_____

Plan and Practice

I will set aside time regularly for prayer, meditation, and spiritual reading and will seek to practice the Presence of God.

_____

_____

_____

By God's grace I will strive mightily against sin and will do deeds of love and mercy that lead to righteousness.

_____

_____

_____

I will seek the gifts of the Holy Spirit, nurturing the fruit and experiencing the joy and power of the Spirit.

_____

_____

_____

I will seek to serve others everywhere I can and will work for justice in all human relationships and social structures.

_____

_____

_____

I will study the Scriptures regularly and share my faith with others as God leads.

_____

_____

_____

I feel scattered, Lord.

Give me an undivided heart to
revere your name.

Psalm 86:11

❧

Set up road markers for yourself,
make yourself guideposts;
consider well the highway,
the road by which you went.

Jeremiah 31:21

Outside the open window
The morning air is all awash with angels.

Richard Wilbur

☙

Our call is to seek the conversion of the
church in the midst of a crumbling empire,
an empire to which the church is now closely
allied. Our question is the old question of
spiritual formation: How is the mind of
Christ formed in us and in our history? . . .
Our only hope is conversion. All the questions
we now face point to that. Anything
less will not be enough.

Jim Wallis

❧

The conversion experience, however it is interpreted, is the moment when at the depths of his being a man says "Yes" to God in his life—the moment when he is cleansed, his life redeemed from his old ways, and his feet set on a new path. At such a time the world seems different because of the shining light that glows within him.

Howard Thurman

Stirrings

Beyond a wholesome discipline, be gentle with yourself.

Max Ehrmann

REFLECTION AND REPORT

In what ways is God making his Presence known to me?

_____
_____
_____
_____

What difficulty or success did I encounter while seeking holiness of heart and life?

_____
_____
_____

What spiritual gifts did the Spirit enable me to exercise?

_____
_____
_____
_____

What opportunities did I have to serve others or work for peace and justice?

_____
_____
_____

How has Scripture shaped the way I think and live?

_____
_____
_____
_____

SPIRITUAL FORMATION GROUP

Name _____

_____

_____

_____

Name _____

_____

_____

_____

Name _____

_____

_____

_____

Name _____

_____

_____

_____

Name _____

_____

_____

_____

Name _____

_____

_____

_____

PLAN AND PRACTICE

I will set aside time regularly for prayer, meditation, and spiritual reading and will seek to practice the Presence of God.

_____

_____

_____

By God's grace I will strive mightily against sin and will do deeds of love and mercy that lead to righteousness.

_____

_____

_____

I will seek the gifts of the Holy Spirit, nurturing the fruit and experiencing the joy and power of the Spirit.

_____

_____

_____

I will seek to serve others everywhere I can and will work for justice in all human relationships and social structures.

_____

_____

_____

I will study the Scriptures regularly and share my faith with others as God leads.

_____

_____

_____

Sources

Evelyn Underhill, *The Spiritual Life* (New York: Harper & Row, 1977), pp. 35–36.

Mother Teresa, *The Love of Christ: Spiritual Counsels, Mother Teresa of Calcutta*, eds. Georges Gorrée and Jean Barbier (San Francisco: Harper & Row, 1982), p. 113.

Josephine Moffett Benton, *The Pace of a Hen* (Philadelphia: Christian Education Press, 1961), p. 48.

Dietrich Bonhoeffer, *Letters and Papers from Prison*, ed. Eberhard Bethge (New York: Macmillan, Collier, 1953), p. 362.

❧

George Müller, *The Life of Trust: Being a Narrative of the Lord's Dealings with George Müller* (Boston: Gould and Lincoln, 1873), pp. 204–5.

Helmut Thielicke, as quoted in Dallas Willard, *The Spirit of the Disciplines* (San Francisco: Harper & Row, 1988), p. 265.

Frederick Buechner, *Wishful Thinking: A Seeker's ABCs* (San Francisco: HarperSanFrancisco, 1973), p. 118.

Paul Tournier, *Reflection on Life's Most Crucial Questions* (New York: Harper & Row, 1976), p. 113.

❧

Hannah Whitall Smith, *The Christian's Secret of a Happy Life* (Waco, TX: Word, 1985), p. 38.

Thomas Kelly, *A Testament of Devotion* (New York: Harper & Brothers, 1941), p. 11.

A. W. Tozer, *Man: The Dwelling Place of God* (Harrisburg, PA: Christian Publications, 1966), p. 44.

George MacDonald, *George MacDonald, 365 Readings*, ed. and preface by C. S. Lewis (New York: Macmillan, 1947), p. 123.

❧

George MacDonald, *George MacDonald, 365 Readings*, p. 138.

Francis de Sales, *An Introduction to the Devout Life*, trans. and ed. John K. Ryan (New York: Doubleday, 1972), p. 90.

Oswald Chambers, *My Utmost for His Highest* (Grand Rapids, MI: Dodd & Mead, Discovery House, 1935), p. 115.

Thomas Merton, as quoted in Esther de Waal, *A Seven Day Journey with Thomas Merton* (Ann Arbor, MI: Servant, 1992), p. 72.

Kathryn A. Yanni, "Renewing Our Minds: The Power of Honest Reflection," *reNews* (November 1993): 8.

Langston Hughes, "Harlem 2," *The Collected Poems of Langston Hughes,* ed. Arnold Rampersad (New York: Knopf, 1994), p. 426.

⁂

Thomas Keating, *Invitation to Love* (Rockport, MA: Element, 1992), p. 73.

Alan Jones, *Passion for Pilgrimage* (San Francisco: Harper & Row, 1989), p. 3.

D. Elton Trueblood, *The Yoke of Christ* (Waco, TX: Word, 1958), pp. 16–17.

Elizabeth O'Connor, *Cry Pain, Cry Hope* (Waco, TX: Word, 1987), p. 84.

⁂

Emily Dickinson, *Final Harvest,* sel. Thomas H. Johnson (Boston: Little, Brown, 1890), p. 208.

Brother Lawrence, *The Practice of the Presence of God* (New York: Revell, 1895), p. 17.

Kelly, *Testament of Devotion*, p. 123.

Benton, *Pace of a Hen*, pp. 79–80.

Thomas Moore, *Care of the Soul* (New York: HarperCollins, HarperPerennial, 1994), p. 14.

⁂

Merton, as quoted in de Waal, *Seven Day Journey*, p. 41.

Elizabeth O'Connor, *Our Many Selves* (New York: Harper & Row, 1971), pp. 107–10.

A. W. Tozer, *The Pursuit of God* (Harrisburg, PA: Christian Publications, n.d.), pp. 9–10.

Moore, *Care of the Soul,* p. 219.

⁂

Luci Shaw, "Notes from a Prayer Getaway," *Virtue* (January/February 1993): 47.

Willard, *Spirit of the Disciplines,* p. 261.

Peter van Breeman, *Certain as the Dawn* (Denville, NJ: Dimension, 1980), p. 37.

Bonhoeffer, *Letters and Papers from Prison*, pp. 361–62.

Francis Schaeffer, *True Spirituality* (Wheaton, IL: Tyndale House, 1971), p. 87.

⁂

George Fox, *Journal of George Fox,* ed. John L. Nickalls (Philadelphia: Philadelphia Yearly Meeting of the Religious Society of Friends, 1985), p. 11.

Anonymous, *The Cloud of Unknowing,* ed. James Walsh (New York: Paulist Press, 1981), p. 265.

Hildegard of Bingen, as quoted in Ronda De Sola Chervin, *Prayers of the Women Mystics* (Ann Arbor, MI: Servant, 1992), p. 21.

Henri Nouwen, Donald P. McNeill, and Douglas A. Morrison, *Compassion: A Reflection on the Christian Life* (Garden City, NY: Doubleday, 1982), pp. 16–17.

Leighton Ford, *The Christian Persuader: A New Look at Evangelism Today* (New York: Harper & Row, 1966), pp. 13–14.

Calvin Miller, *A Requiem for Love* (Dallas, TX: Word, 1989), p. 42.

❧

William Penn, *Fruits of Solitude* (Chicago: Donnelley, 1906), p. 83.

Jones, *Passion for Pilgrimage,* pp. 36–37.

Tozer, *Pursuit of God,* p. 127.

Chambers, *My Utmost for His Highest,* p. 118.

George MacDonald, *George MacDonald, 365 Readings,* p. 121.

❧

Thomas à Kempis, *The Imitation of Christ* (Chicago: Moody, 1958), p. 107.

Anonymous, *The Way of a Pilgrim,* trans. Helen Bacovcin (New York: Doubleday, Image, 1978), p. 147.

William Law, *A Serious Call to a Devout and Holy Life* (Philadelphia: Westminster, 1940), p. 138.

William Blake, "The Little Black Boy," *The Portable Blake,* ed. Alfred Kazin (New York: Viking, Penguin, 1946), p. 86.

❧

Willard, *Spirit of the Disciplines,* p. 138.

Tozer, *Man: the Dwelling Place of God,* p. 66.

Merton, as quoted in de Waal, *Seven Day Journey,* p. 32.

Tozer, *Pursuit of God,* pp. 13–14.

❧

Oswald Chambers, *The Psychology of Redemption* (London: Oswald Chambers Publications and Marshall, Morgan and Scott, 1955), pp. 26–27.

Gregory of Nyssa, *Life of Moses*, ed. Richard Payne (New York: Paulist, 1978), p. 12.

Jones, *Passion for Pilgrimage*, p. 106.

John H. Westerhoff and John D. Eusden, *The Spiritual Life* (New York: Seabury, 1982), pp. 75–76.

Miller, *Requiem for Love*, p. 41.

❧

Robert Robinson, "Come, Thou Fount of Every Blessing," *Hymns for the Family of God* (Nashville, TN: Paragon, 1976), p. 318.

Bonhoeffer, *Letters and Papers from Prison*, p. 10.

Henri Nouwen, *With Open Hands* (Notre Dame, IN: Ave Maria, 1972), p. 64.

Rainer Maria Rilke, *Letters to a Young Poet*, trans. M. D. Herter Norton (New York: Norton, 1934), p. 35.

❧

François Fénelon, *Christian Perfection* (Minneapolis, MN: Bethany, 1975), pp. 28–29.

Dag Hammarskjöld, *Markings*, trans. Leif Sjöberg and W. H. Auden (New York: Knopf, 1964), p. 122.

Willard, *Spirit of the Disciplines*, p. 263.

William Penn, *No Cross, No Crown*, rev. and ed. Ronald Selleck (Richmond, IN: Friends United Press, 1981), p. xviii.

Evelyn Underhill, *The Ways of the Spirit*, ed. Grace Adolphsen Brame (New York: Crossroad, 1990), p. 35.

❧

William Penn, "The Rise and Progress of the People Called Quakers," a preface of the *Journal of George Fox*, written in 1694. *Passages from the Life and Writings of William Penn*, col. and ed. Thomas Cope (Philadelphia: Friends' Bookstore, 304 Arch Street, 1882), p. 417.

T. S. Eliot, *Collected Poems 1909–1962* (New York: Harcourt Brace, 1963), p. 157.

William Law, *Daily Readings with William Law*, ed. Robert Llewelyn and Edward Moss (Springfield, IL: Templegate, 1987), p. 41.

Jacques Ellul, *The Presence of the Kingdom* (Colorado Springs, CO: Helmers & Howard, 1989), p. 47.

George MacDonald, *George MacDonald, 365 Readings*, p. 47.

❧

Francis de Sales, *Introduction to the Devout Life*, pp. 52, 54.

Andrew Murray, *Abide in Christ* (St. Louis, MO: Bible Memory Association, n.d.),
    pp. 66–67.

John Woolman, *The Journal of John Woolman* (Secaucus, NJ: Citadel, 1961), p. 229.

Augustine, *The Confessions of Saint Augustine*, trans. E. M. Blaiklock (Nashville: Thomas
    Nelson, 1983), p. 15.

Madeleine L'Engle, "Annunciation," *The Irrational Season* (New York: Seabury, 1977),
    p. 27.

❧

Kelly, *Testament of Devotion*, p. 29.

John Climacus, as quoted in *Way of a Pilgrim*, p. 146.

Lewis B. Smedes, *Forgive and Forget* (New York: Simon & Schuster, Pocket Books, 1984),
    p. 12.

Law, *Daily Readings with William Law*, p. 49.

❧

Alexandra Stoddard, *Living Beautifully Together* (New York: Avon, 1989), p. 7.

George Herbert, as quoted in Jones, *Passion for Pilgrimage*, p. 2.

Westminster Shorter Catechism, *The Constitution of the United Presbyterian Church in the
    United States of America*. Part 1, *Book of Confessions* (Philadelphia: The General
    Assembly of the United Presbyterian Church in the United States of America, 1966),
    p. 7.001–.011.

Teresa of Ávila, as quoted in Benton, *Pace of a Hen*, p. 1.

❧

Mother Teresa, *Love: A Fruit Always in Season*, sel. and ed. Dorothy S. Hunt (San Francisco:
    Ignatius Press, 1987), p. 83.

Francis de Sales, *Introduction to the Devout Life*, pp. 43–44.

Brennan Manning, *Lion and Lamb* (Old Tappan, NJ: Revell, Chosen, 1986), p. 110.

Madeleine L'Engle, "Epiphany," *The Irrational Season*, p. 39.

Madame Guyon, *Experience God Through Prayer* (Springdale, PA: Whitaker House, 1984),
    p. 17.

※

Meister Eckhart, as quoted in Kelly, *Testament of Devotion*, p. 29.

Hammarskjöld, *Markings*, p. 146.

Brother Lawrence, as quoted in Benton, *Pace of a Hen*, p. 88.

John H. Yoder, *The Politics of Jesus: Vicit Agnus Noster* (Grand Rapids, MI: Eerdmans, 1972), p. 250.

Manning, *Lion and Lamb*, p. 63.

※

Richard Wilbur, "Love Calls Us to the Things of This World," *New and Collected Poems* (New York: Harcourt Brace Jovanovich, 1988), p. 233.

Jim Wallis, *The Call to Conversion: Recovering the Gospel for These Times* (San Francisco: Harper & Row, 1981), p. xviii.

Thurman, *Disciplines of the Spirit*, pp. 23–24.

Max Ehrmann, "Desiderata" (Boston: Bruce Humphries, 1948).